# Working for Myself

WITHDRAWN

# OTHER PEOPLE'S PETS

*Tana Reiff*

**AGS®**

American Guidance Service, Inc.
Circle Pines, Minnesota 55014-1796
1-800-328-2560

## Working for Myself

*Cooking for a Crowd*
*You Call, We Haul*
*Your Kids and Mine*
*The Flower Man*
*The Green Team*
*Clean as a Whistle*
*Beauty and the Business*
*Handy All Around*
*Crafting a Business*

Cover Illustration: James Balkovek
Cover Design: Ina McInnis
Text Designer: Diann Abbott

Library of Congress Catalog Number: 94-076143
ISBN 0-7854-1113-5 (Previously ISBN 1-56103-905-5)
Product Number 40833
Printed in the United States of America
A 0 9 8 7 6 5 4 3 2

# CONTENTS

## Chapter

**C H A P T E R   1**

# A Love for Animals

Sam was an old mutt with the kindest dog heart in the world. Now he lay dying. Sam had been Ginny's best pal since she was a little girl.

She remembered the day she found him. He was in a box by the side of the road. A sign on the box said: FREE PUPPY. Ginny took him home. She loved him right away.

"What's that little rag?" her mom said

when she first saw the dirty little puppy.

"Oh, please, can we keep him?" Ginny begged her mom.

"Give him a bath," her mom said. "We'll decide after he's cleaned up."

Ginny got a bucket and filled it with water. She rubbed soap all over the puppy. He stood still and let Ginny wash him. Then he jumped around and shook himself. Ginny dried him with a towel. The puppy looked like a soft ball of fur.

"Please, Mom?" she asked again. Sam went over to Ginny's mom. He looked right into her eyes. That look melted her heart.

"How can I say no?" her mom laughed.

All the time Ginny was growing up, Sam was her buddy. He grew much too large for a bucket bath, but he always had a baby face. He seemed almost like a brother to Ginny, even though she had two real brothers. Sam loved her back— no matter what.

Now, Sam was old and very sick. Ginny

knew he couldn't last much longer. She stroked his fur. She fed him out of her hand. The old boy could hardly lift his head.

Then Sam closed his eyes for the last time. He was gone.

Ginny dug a grave in the backyard. She marked it with a stone. She painted SAM on it in big letters.

"Why don't you get another dog?" Ginny's mom asked her.

"There can never be another Sam," Ginny said.

Then one day Ginny's friend Eva called. "I'm going away to visit my boyfriend," Eva said. "I don't want to leave my dog in a kennel. She would much rather stay home. Could you come by every day and feed her?"

Ginny wasn't sure she was ready even to take care of another dog. But she understood how Eva felt. She would have hated to leave Sam in a kennel. So she said, "OK."

"Stop over for the key and stay a while," said Eva. "That way Roberta can get to know you. Of course, I want to pay you for this."

"You don't have to pay me," Ginny told her friend.

"Come on!" Eva said. "I'd pay plenty for a kennel. Don't put up a fight. Just get over here."

Ginny put on her coat and drove over to Eva's house.

Roberta was a little white furry thing, not at all like Sam. When Ginny walked in, the dog sniffed her up and down. She knew Ginny right away. She just kept on sniffing anyway.

Eva was painting her nails bright pink. "If that dog touches my hands, I'll have to do my nails all over again!" she said.

"Roberta looks really pretty," said Ginny, petting the soft fur.

"I just finished clipping her today," said Eva. The dog sniffed her hand.

"I see you clipped your dog's nails, too," Ginny laughed.

Eva showed Ginny where she kept the food. She showed how much to feed Roberta. She gave Ginny a leash so she could walk Roberta around the block.

Then Ginny noticed Eva's plants. "Do you want me to water your plants while you're away?" Ginny asked. "I might as well. And I could bring in your newspaper and mail, too."

"Great!" said Eva. "I won't have a thing to worry about! And will you be sure to give my baby some TLC every day?"

Ginny picked up Roberta and rubbed her head. "That goes without saying," she said. "Love is part of the deal!"

"You really *do* love animals, don't you?" Eva asked.

"Yeah," said Ginny. "I guess I do. I thought I only loved Sam. But maybe I loved Sam so much because I love animals so much."

"You know, there are people who do

pet-sitting for a living," said Eva.

"Really? They go into people's homes to take care of their pets?"

"Oh, yeah," said Eva. "Lots of people have pets. And lots of people worry when they plan a trip. They don't want their pets to leave home when they go away. Look in the phone book. There are quite a few pet-sitters."

"Really?" said Ginny.

"That would be a good job for you," said Eva. "You're cut out for it. That's why I asked you."

"I have my night job," Ginny said.

"That crummy job? Heck, you could pet-sit during the day and still keep your job."

"That does give me an idea," Ginny said.

Eva gave Ginny a key to the front door. "Here," Eva said. "Guard this key with your life. I hope everything goes fine with my baby. I know she's in good hands."

"Don't worry," said Ginny. "And I'll

think about what you said. If sitting Roberta goes OK, maybe one thing will lead to another."

"Well, we'll just see, won't we?" laughed Eva.

Ginny stopped by Eva's place the next day and again the next. The third day she made a second trip. She was getting to like these little visits. Pet-sitting didn't seem like work at all.

**CHAPTER 2**

# Something to Work On

Eva's dog was little and jumpy. She was no good at playing "stick." All she wanted to do was dash around like a rabbit. She was very different from Sam. But Ginny found herself liking this dog. She began to wonder if she could learn to like cats, too.

Her chance came after Eva came home. "You did a great job with Roberta," Eva told Ginny. "My aunt is leaving town soon. She has a cat. Can I give her your phone number?"

"I guess so," Ginny said. "I don't know much about cats, though."

"I'll tell you the main difference," said Eva. "A cat has a mind of its own. And most cats have litter boxes. If you ask me, those things are no fun at all to clean out. But then neither are dog's ears, and you do that."

Eva always made Ginny laugh. "I don't think I would mind cleaning a litter box," she said.

So she made plans to take care of Eva's aunt's cat.

But before the time came, Ginny made some phone calls. She found four pet-sitters listed in the phone book. She called them all.

"I'm thinking about getting into the pet-sitting business," Ginny told each one. "Can you tell me a little about it?"

One pet-sitter wasn't willing to talk. He said he didn't care to share the secrets of his successful business.

One pet-sitter was too busy to talk. But she said there was plenty of work in town for another pet-sitter.

The third pet-sitter gave Ginny some tips on buying insurance. He said that two types were important—liability insurance and bonding.

Suppose something happened to the pet-owner's house. Suppose something happened to the pet. Suppose the pet-sitter lost the door key and new locks had to be put in. Suppose the pet-owner sued the pet-sitter. Even if the pet-sitter did nothing wrong, getting sued would cost a lot of money. A pet-sitter, he said, needed liability insurance.

And a pet-sitter needed bonding, the man went on. Some people might worry that a pet-sitter would steal things. With bonding, they could rest easy. The bonding company would pay for anything that was missing. Then the pet-sitter would have to pay back the bonding company. A pet-sitter, he said, needed to be bonded.

"I'll look into liability insurance and bonding," Ginny said.

Ginny couldn't thank the man enough.

She got more tips from the last person on the list. This young woman had started her own pet-sitting business in high school. Now she had five people working for her. That way she always had someone to fill in when needed. The workers did most of the pet-sitting. The owner spent most of her time running the business.

This woman told Ginny to keep track of every mile she drove. She told her to write down every penny she spent on the business. She also said that most of her work came by word-of-mouth. One person would tell another, she said, and so on and so on. She gave Ginny ideas for how to start that word-of-mouth.

The next day Ginny got out of bed a little early. She ate breakfast faster than usual. She skipped the morning talk shows. She got in the car and drove to a pet shop.

"My name is Ginny Carr," she told the friendly man behind the counter. "I was wondering—does anyone ever ask you about pet-sitting?"

"As a matter of fact, they do," said the man.

"Well, I'm looking for pet-sitting work," said Ginny. "I have another job, but it starts at 5:00. I can take care of the pets during the day."

"You're welcome to put up a sign," said the man. He pointed to the bulletin board next to the door. He even gave Ginny a piece of paper and a pen.

She wrote *PET-SITTING* at the top of the paper. Under that she wrote: *Going away? Leave your pet in good hands. CALL ME*. Then she wrote her phone number sideways across the bottom ten times. She tore the paper between each phone number. That way, people could tear off the phone number to take along with them.

"Thanks a lot," Ginny told the man at the pet store.

"I hope you get some business out of it," he said.

Next, Ginny went to an animal doctors' office. They let her put up a sign, too. But the vet's helper said, "Really, it would be better if we could hand out your business cards."

"I don't have any business cards," Ginny said. "I guess I should get some made."

"That would be a good idea," said the vet's helper.

Ginny's last stop was a travel office. She thought that people going on vacation might want to know about pet-sitting.

"Oh, yes," said the woman at the travel office. "People often ask me about pet-sitting. Now I'll know what to tell them."

When Ginny got home her mom asked

where she had been all day. Ginny told her. Then she added, "I hope you don't mind answering the phone for me when I'm not here."

Her mom laughed. "Gosh, no," she said. "It sounds like a good idea to me."

Ginny got ready for work. As she was going out the door a picture of Sam popped into her head. Tears came into her eyes. But then something came to her. This was the first she had thought of Sam all day.

**C H A P T E R  3**

# First Real Job

There was a note on the kitchen table when Ginny got home from work. "Call Mrs. Hobbs. 555-2388."

Ginny looked at the clock. It was too late to call now. But first thing in the morning, she called the number.

Mrs. Hobbs asked a lot of questions. After all, she just *loved* her dog. She didn't want to leave her with just *anyone*.

"I got your name at the vet's office,"

Mrs. Hobbs began. "How long have you been in the pet-sitting business?"

"To tell the truth, I'm just getting started," Ginny answered. "But I took good care of my own dog for 14 years. And I took care of two other people's pets since he died."

"How do I know I can count on you?" Mrs. Hobbs asked.

"I love animals," said Ginny. "I'll treat your pet like my own. I have another job, and I never miss work. Tell you what. I'll give you my friend Eva's number. I took care of her dog last month. She knows how I am about going to my night job. She'll put in a good word for me."

Mrs. Hobbs hung up. She called back in five minutes. "Your friend gives you high marks, all right. Why don't you come over and meet my Muffy?"

*Muffy.* Ginny couldn't stand that name. It made her think of a spoiled little mama's baby. But this might be a test. If she could take care of a dog named Muffy, she could take care of anything.

Ginny felt nervous as soon as she walked into Mrs. Hobbs' house. She could see this would be a fussy customer. Everything was set up like a show house. There was not a speck of dust anywhere. Ginny was almost afraid to walk on the carpet. And Muffy was wearing a jacket!

"Now, Muffy must be fed twice a day," said Mrs. Hobbs. "So I will pay you to make two visits each day, morning and evening."

"I'm sorry, but I go to work at 5:00," Ginny broke in.

Mrs. Hobbs looked shocked. "Very well," she said. "You can stop by on your way to work. Now, in the morning Muffy eats the wet food. In the evening, give her the dry food. If you give her dry food in the morning, she'll choke. And make sure she has fresh water in her dish at all times."

"Of course," said Ginny.

"Muffy and I take two walks every

day," Mrs. Hobbs went on. "We walk one time around the block. Don't forget to put on her jacket. We wouldn't want her to get a chill, would we? Her leash is hanging in the hall closet."

Muffy jumped out of Mrs. Hobbs' arms.

"Here, girl!" Ginny called to the dog. She wanted to see if Muffy would come to her. She wanted Muffy to get to know her before Mrs. Hobbs went away.

Muffy came right over. Ginny picked her up and patted the fur on her little head. Muffy looked like a cousin of Eva's dog. But Eva's dog didn't wear a jacket.

"I can't believe she took to you so fast," said Mrs. Hobbs. "I guess she won't miss me so much after all." For a moment Muffy's owner looked a little sad. But then she perked up. "Very well. That's why I hired a pet-sitter, isn't it?"

"Where are you going?" Ginny asked Mrs. Hobbs. "I'll need the address and phone number."

"I'm visiting my sister in France," Mrs.

Hobbs said. She wrote down her sister's name, address, and phone number. Then she handed the paper to Ginny. "Of course, it wouldn't do much good to call France, would it?" she laughed. "I couldn't just come running home anyway, now could I?"

"And a key," said Ginny. "I'll need a key to get in."

"Oh, of course," said Mrs. Hobbs. "But how do I know I can trust you with my house key?"

"I'm getting insurance," said Ginny. "By the way, I'd be happy to bring in your newspaper and mail every day."

"Wonderful!" said Mrs. Hobbs. "Then I won't have to bother my neighbor about that. And while you're at it, would you please water my plants on Saturday?"

"Sure," said Ginny.

"One more thing," said Mrs. Hobbs. She reached for a little bottle. "Muffy needs her drops every morning. Just two drops on the tongue. She's very good about taking her drops."

There were many things for Ginny to remember. The key. The walk around the block. Wet food in the morning, dry in the evening. Newspaper and mail. Water the plants. Two drops every morning.

As soon as Ginny got home, she wrote it all down. Then she got a bright idea. She worked out a contract form for people to fill in. That way, she would never forget to ask all the important questions. She would always know when and what to feed the pet. Everything about the animal would be written down in black and white. At the bottom, she put a line for the pet-owner's name.

And she sent off two checks. One was for liability insurance and one for bonding.

Ginny could see that pet-sitting was a real business. She didn't want to make any mistakes.

**C H A P T E R   4**

# Troubles with Muffy

Ginny's visits with Muffy went fine for the first three days. She took the dog for walks and always put the jacket on her. "You look pretty silly to me," Ginny said. "But you're supposed to wear your jacket when we go out, so that's what you'll do."

Ginny followed all of the other directions, too. She gave Muffy two drops on the tongue every morning. She watered the plants. She did everything on the list and she did it right.

But on the fourth morning, Ginny forgot to bring her list of chores. "Is it dry food or wet food in the morning?" she asked Muffy. The dog didn't answer. Ginny gave her the dry food. Muffy began to choke.

Ginny picked up the dog and turned her upside down. But Muffy was still choking.

"Oh, no!" Ginny said to herself. "I forgot to ask Mrs. Hobbs the name of Muffy's vet."

Then Ginny remembered where Mrs. Hobbs had heard about her. Ginny had visited only one vet's office. But now she couldn't remember the doctors' names. She found Mrs. Hobbs' phone book. In the yellow pages she looked up *Veterinarians*. She spotted a name she knew and called the number.

The woman who answered told Ginny to bring Muffy in right away. There was no time to waste. With food stuck in her throat, Muffy could hardly breathe. She could die.

Ginny picked up the little dog and ran to her car. In four minutes she was at the vet's office. The doctor knew just what to do. A chunk of food popped out of Muffy's mouth. She was all right.

When Ginny got home, she added another line on her contract form. VETERINARIAN TO CALL IN CASE OF AN EMERGENCY, she wrote.

Mrs. Hobbs was supposed to return on Sunday afternoon. In the morning Ginny visited Muffy as usual. It was Ginny's last day on the job. Mrs. Hobbs had not said what to do with the key. Ginny took the key out of her pocket. She started to lay it on the kitchen table. Then she stopped herself.

What if Mrs. Hobbs didn't get home today after all? Ginny decided to hold on to the key—just in case. Sometime tomorrow she could stop by to return it.

On Monday morning, Ginny went to

Mrs. Hobbs' house. She rang the bell, even though she had the key. No answer. Then Ginny heard Muffy. The little dog was crying on the other side of the door.

Ginny used the key. No one was home, except poor Muffy. The little dog was hungry. Ginny knew that she needed her drops. She went inside to take care of her.

Why hadn't Mrs. Hobbs called her? Then Ginny wondered if Mrs. Hobbs had lost her phone number. It was strange that she hadn't called.

Later in the day, Ginny returned for the second visit. This time, Mrs. Hobbs was there—and she was very upset. But she wasn't angry with Ginny.

"I'm so glad you kept the key!" said Mrs. Hobbs. "My plane was late. It would have been terrible if you couldn't get into the house today. In fact, dear, I'd like you to keep the key. I'm sure I'll use you again. And besides, I'll always know that you have it."

Mrs. Hobbs paid Ginny for a full extra

day. And she gave her a nice big tip, too.

Ginny went home and added another line to the contract form: PLEASE CALL GINNY AS SOON AS YOU RETURN HOME. That way she could be sure that a pet would never be left alone again.

Everything had gone fine with Eva's dog. But Ginny wasn't happy with the Muffy job. There had been so many problems.

"Every business runs into some problems," Eva told Ginny. "But at least you worked things out. Sometimes you just have to learn the hard way."

"I'll say," Ginny said.

"So when are you going to quit your crummy job?" Eva asked.

"That's a long way off," said Ginny. "But it's something to work for."

## CHAPTER 5

# All Kinds of Animals

Ginny's next adventure starred a parrot named Pete. It was her first bird-sitting job.

Pete's family said that he was really a person. He only *looked* like a bird. He did talk. He had been taught to say some smart things, like "Move it, dummy!" and "Think again!"

And sometimes Pete came out with strange sounds of his own. Maybe his owners were right. Maybe he really *was* a person. Anyway, Ginny thought that Pete was very funny.

One day Ginny went to see Pete. But the parrot was gone! The door to his cage hung open. The cage was empty. And the house was quiet.

"Oh, no," Ginny said. "They told me how much that bird cost. Plus, they think he's a person. If he got away, they're going to kill me!"

She began to search the house. She looked all over, upstairs and down. She looked in every closet. She looked high. She looked low. She even looked in every bush in the backyard.

No Pete.

Ginny sat down on the sofa and cried. Then she thought she heard a noise. She stopped crying to listen. But she didn't hear anything. The sound must have been her own sobbing. She began to cry again.

"I never should have agreed to take on

a bird," she said out loud.

Then she heard the noise again. But this time when she stopped to listen, she heard the words, "Up here!"

It had to be Pete. It just *had* to be. But where was his voice coming from?

"Up here!" Ginny heard again.

She tried to follow the sound. It led her up the steps to the second floor.

"Move it, dummy!" No question about it. This was Pete talking.

The noise led Ginny into the upstairs bathroom. It was the one room she hadn't searched. There was Pete. He was perched on top of the shower head.

"Up here, dummy!" he chirped.

"I don't believe this!" Ginny said. She put out her hand. Pete jumped on. She carried the parrot back to his cage.

"I guess you don't like being in a cage all the time," Ginny said to Pete. "But you're a *bird*. I don't care what they say. You look like a bird. You sound like a bird. You eat like a bird. A very smart bird, for sure—but you *are* a bird. So don't you forget it, OK?"

"Think again!" Pete said.

Ginny laughed. She was glad the bird was all right.

When Pete's owners got home, she told them what had happened.

"Oh, he does that all the time," they said. "We should have told you."

That day Ginny added yet another question to the contract form: DOES YOUR PET HAVE ANY UNUSUAL HABITS? It would have been nice to know about Pete's little habit right from the start.

Then there was Pipper the cat. He would not eat unless his dish was placed straight in line with the door. His owners wrote this on the form. But Ginny didn't believe it until she saw it for herself.

As a test, she turned Pipper's dish sideways. She knew that the cat was hungry. But he walked away from the dish and left the room. A few minutes later, he came back in. The dish was still sideways. Pipper pushed the dish but he couldn't get it straight.

Finally Ginny put the dish straight in line with the door. Pipper ate as if there were no tomorrow.

When he was finished, Ginny picked him up and gave him a hug. She sat down with the cat on her lap. He purred and purred as she stroked his fur.

"You miss your friends, don't you?" she asked Pipper. He let out a meow. Ginny was sure that he was answering her question.

Then Pipper fell asleep. Ginny lifted him off her lap and laid him down. It was time to go, and she still had to clean the litter box.

Ginny's favorite job of all was walking dogs. She liked to walk anyway—and dogs always made good company. "I can't believe I'm getting paid for this," she would say to herself.

She got to know many different kinds

of animals. One time she took care of a pair of rabbits. Another job was for two turtles and a hamster. Once she even pet-sat a snake! That was one kind of animal she had never liked. But pretty soon, her fear of snakes was gone. She even learned to wear the snake around her neck!

Once, Ginny took care of a horse. She had to brush the huge animal every day. She fed it sugar out of her hand.

But when the call came to take care of a pet pig, Ginny drew the line. She had heard that pigs made good pets. But she just didn't want to see for herself. "I'm sorry," Ginny told the caller. "I don't do pigs."

Every business has its limits.

## CHAPTER 6

# A Growing Business

Ginny's whole plan seemed to be coming together. She kept a date book. Now she always knew where she was going. Every day was different.

She put a tag on every key she got. She marked the tag with a number, not an address. In case it got lost, no one but Ginny would know which door it fit.

At each home, Ginny brought in the mail and newspaper on the way in. Once inside, she fed the animal first. Then, while the animal was eating, she watered plants and cleaned up any mess the animal had made. After that it was TLC time. Dogs got a walk. Cats got a lap.

Before she left, Ginny wrote a little report for the owners. Then she went around the house and turned on lights. She chose different lights each day. From the outside it looked as if the family was at home.

Back in the car, Ginny wrote down the number of miles she had gone. When the whole job was finished, she went back to each house. That's when she returned the key and got paid.

Each job was different, but one thing was always the same. The animals were always happy to see Ginny. They knew that if Ginny was there, they had a friend. And they knew she would be back again soon.

Word spread about Ginny's pet-sitting. She was getting lots of work. Within a few months, she was so busy she didn't know what to do. She was on the move most of every day. Then she went on to her night job. Some days she didn't even have enough time to sleep. Business seemed to be almost *too* good. Ginny was getting very tired.

A few weeks before Thanksgiving, the phone started ringing off the wall. "I wish you'd buy an answering machine," Ginny's mom said. "I'm getting tired of answering this phone all day and night!"

"I will," Ginny told her.

"Better yet, I wish you'd get your own phone number," said her mom. "This line is tied up so much, my friends can't get through. And your brothers have to go out to a payphone to make a call!"

Two weeks before Thanksgiving, the phone never stopped ringing. People were getting ready to go away for a long weekend. It seemed that half the town needed a pet-sitter!

Ginny's thoughts were a jumble. She

didn't know what to do. She already had more work than she could handle. She even turned some business away. It would cost money to put in her own phone line. She was so tired that she couldn't think straight.

That's when her friend Eva said, "Don't you see? It's time to quit your crummy night job!"

Ginny broke out in a smile. She knew that Eva was right. But quitting a job is a big thing to decide about. She wouldn't have any more paid sick leave or vacation days. And she would have to buy her own medical insurance. Before Ginny did anything crazy, she had to study some numbers.

She looked over her records. She checked to see just how much money she was making.

Then she added up what she might make if she *didn't* turn away work. With the holidays coming up, she could be very busy. But what about after that? She was sure there would be slow times during the long winter months.

"Big deal!" said Eva. "What's the worst thing that can happen? You find another crummy job!"

Ginny wished she could be as care-free as Eva. But in her heart she knew that Eva was right.

"That's it! I'm going to quit my job!" Ginny said.

That night she gave her boss two weeks' notice. Starting the next day, Ginny stopped turning down pet-sitting work. Instead, she took every job that came her way. She had her own phone put in. For now, she wrote in the new number on her business cards. Later she would have new cards printed. She felt very pleased with what she was doing.

She loved to get up in the morning, throw on old clothes, and go out to visit animals. Pets didn't care about what she wore.

But her problems were not over.

**C H A P T E R  7**

# Holiday Blues

Thanksgiving weekend was very, very busy. Ginny had to eat her turkey dinner in 15 minutes. She had 10 more animals to visit that day. She was so busy, she forgot to cut Brandy the poodle's nails. It was written out on the contract form. Ginny simply forgot.

Brandy's family got home on Sunday. They called Ginny right away. But they had more to say than, "We're home now."

"You forgot to cut Brandy's nails!" cried the angry voice on the phone.

"I did?" said Ginny. "I'm sorry."

"You'd *better* be sorry!" the woman screamed.

"Gee, do a few extra days really matter?" Ginny asked.

"When Brandy's nails get long, they scratch our wood floors," said the woman. "A poodle's nails are very sharp!"

"I see. Well, I'm really sorry." Ginny thought the people were making a big deal out of this. But her pet-sitting service was a business. In business, they say that the customer is always right. "Did Brandy's nails scratch your floors?" Ginny asked.

"Well, no," said the woman. "But that was just lucky."

"I'll be more careful next time," said Ginny. "I promise."

"There won't *be* a next time!" the woman shouted.

Ginny didn't argue. She didn't need

customers like this. You win some, you lose some, she said to herself.

At the end of the weekend, Ginny ran into one more problem. It happened at the last place she visited on Sunday night. As she got to the door, she wondered why the house was dark. She had left two lights on.

Ginny stepped inside and turned on the hall light. When she looked into the living room, she couldn't believe her eyes. Two lamps lay broken on the floor. A flower vase was in tiny pieces in a puddle. The place was a mess. The dog had turned over everything in sight. He had even chewed the chair legs.

Just then the dog crawled out from behind the sofa. He held his head down. He knew he had done something very wrong.

Ginny had a few words with the dog. "Bad boy!" she told him. "Look what you've done!" Then she patted him on the head. Her voice turned soft. "You were lonely, weren't you?" she said to him.

With that, she cleaned up the mess. She wrote down what happened in her report to the owners. Then she called the insurance company.

It was quite a weekend. The problems were no fun, but most of it went fine. On Monday, after Ginny got her money, she added it all up. Those little problems had been worth it. Ginny couldn't believe how much money she had made.

The end-of-year holidays made Thanksgiving look like a picnic. By the second week in December, Ginny was all booked up. Even without her night job, she couldn't take on any more work. She asked Eva to help out during this busy time.

Eva had wanted a part-time job for the holidays. Instead she worked for Ginny. To learn what to do, she went along with Ginny on a few jobs. Ginny had to make sure that Eva would do all right on her own.

Ginny told Eva how much she could pay her for each visit. That was fine with Eva.

The two of them got to work. Ginny told Eva that Hanukkah started early that year. People would be going away by the second week in December. There would be no let-up in business all through the month. And the phone calls kept coming. Ginny and Eva were both having a lot of fun. But they were busy all the time.

The day before Christmas it started to snow. Hour after hour it snowed and snowed. By Christmas morning everything was covered in a thick white blanket. Ginny looked out the window. Her car was buried deep in the snow. Her heart sank. "Now what do I do?" she wondered.

The family had three snow shovels — one each for Ginny and her two brothers. Ginny got out the snow shovels and called the boys. "You've got to help me!"

she cried. "If we all dig together, I can get my car out!"

She was lucky her brothers liked her. They put on their coats and went outside to help. The three of them worked hard. An hour later, the snowplow came through. Ginny backed her car into the street.

Then Ginny thought of Eva. Eva's car was terrible in snow. Even if she could dig it out, it would be no good on the road. Ginny went back inside to call her friend.

Nothing worried Eva. "No problem," she told Ginny. "The bus is running. I'll just put on my boots and take the bus. I'll get as close as I can to my houses and then I'll walk."

"You're great!" Ginny said. "But listen. We'll be lucky to make it to every place even one time today. Don't even think about doing any second trips. Just give the animals extra food and water. And don't walk any dogs, OK?"

"OK."

Ginny made all 15 of her visits that day. Eva did all 10 of hers. At some places they had to trudge through snowdrifts just to get to the door. But they made it. They *had* to. They couldn't let down the pets. Those animals were just too important.

Long after dark, Ginny got home. She was tired and hungry. Her mom heated up what was left of Christmas dinner. Ginny enjoyed every bite of it, even if she had to eat alone.

It didn't snow on New Year's Day. It was easy for Ginny to make all of her visits. But she missed watching the football games with her brothers. Ginny thought about it. She decided that giving up some fun was part of running a business. It was a price Ginny was willing to pay.

# Time to Sell

Ginny's business was a whole different story after the holidays. Some people took winter vacations. But most stayed home during the cold weather. It was true that Ginny needed a break. And she had expected business to slow down. But she never expected things to be *this* slow.

It was time to put the word out again.

Ginny took out an ad in the phone book. She made new signs and took them all over. She took them to food stores. She put them on any bulletin board she could find.

She also went back to the pet store, the vet's office, and the travel office. She wanted to make sure that everyone knew she was still around.

She spent extra time at the travel office. "A lot of single people take winter vacations," said the woman there. "They don't have children in school, you see. They're free to go away whenever they can take the time."

"Let's make a deal," said Ginny. "You give my card to your single customers. You stamp your business name on the back of each card. If they show me their card, I'll pay you for your trouble."

"That's fair," said the woman.

Ginny got quite a few jobs from that deal. It was worth paying a little to get that winter work.

Then Ginny thought some more about who would need a pet-sitter. She thought of working couples with no children. Don't their pets get lonely? Maybe they would pay for someone to look in on their pets during the day.

So Ginny went around to all kinds of businesses. She gave out her card at offices all over town. Sure enough, she got more work that way.

One day, Mrs. Hobbs called. Ginny had watched Muffy three different times. She thought Mrs. Hobbs was calling to ask her again. But instead Mrs. Hobbs told Ginny that Muffy had died.

"My dear, she choked on her dry food!" Mrs. Hobbs explained. "And in the *evening*! Can you believe that? Why, she was in better hands with you than she was with me."

Ginny sent Mrs. Hobbs a sympathy card. She knew how much Muffy had meant to her. She wrote, "Muffy was my first real job. I'll never forget her."

Not long after, Mrs. Hobbs bought a puppy. She called Ginny and said, "That card meant so much to me, dear. I'd like you to come and sit my new Buffy. I got a little boy this time!"

Ginny took Buffy a gift of little chewy sticks to cut his teeth on. Mrs. Hobbs was very pleased. It made good sense to keep her customers happy.

Then one day Ginny got a call from a pet shampoo company. The man asked her if she might want to sell good pet shampoo. She could also sell brushes and combs for cats and dogs.

"You can make lots of extra money with our products," said the man. "Everything we make is so good it will sell itself!"

"Do I have to buy anything up front?" Ginny wanted to know.

"Not a thing," the man promised. "We give you a starter kit. All you do is show it to your customers. Let them try the products. Then just take their orders and call them in to us. The products will be delivered the very next day."

"Sounds like I can't lose," said Ginny.

"There is no way you can lose," said the man. "With our pet products, everybody wins. You, me, and most of all the pets!"

So Ginny began selling the pet shampoo, brushes, and combs. She made a dollar here and a dollar there. It all added up.

Ginny made one more business move during the slow winter. She gave her pet-sitting service a name. She believed that a real business name might add something.

She thought up many names. She checked with the state. Other pet-sitting services were already using some of her ideas. *Pet Keeper, Critter Sitter, Animal Watcher, Home Pet Care*—they were all taken.

Ginny thought and thought about what makes a good name for a business. For one thing, the name should be easy to remember. For another, it should be different—but not *too* different. Mostly it should tell what was really special about her pet-sitting service.

Then Ginny came up with just the right name. No one was using it yet. From now on her business would be known as *Tender Loving Pet Care*, or *TLPC*.

Ginny filled out some forms. By law, she had to place a business notice in the newspaper classified section.

Now she had to get new business cards. The new ones said *TLPC* in big letters across the top. Under that were the words *TENDER LOVING PET CARE*. On the side was a paw print. And at the bottom were her name and new phone number.

Ginny sat back in her chair and looked out the kitchen window. She saw patches of green grass poking up through the melting snow. Spring was on its way!

Ginny now had an ad in the phone book and new signs. She was paying the travel office for talking to singles, and leaving her card at offices. She was sending cards and selling pet shampoo. And now she had a new business name. Ginny the pet-sitter was ready for anything. No kind of weather could slow her down now.

# Pet Taxi

One of Ginny's very best shampoo customers was Mrs. Hobbs. "Buffy won't let me wash him with anything else," she said. So Ginny made a lot of trips to Mrs. Hobbs' house just to drop off shampoo.

One day, just like always, Ginny was bringing Mrs. Hobbs some bottles of pet shampoo. But this time, she found Mrs. Hobbs with a cast on her leg. "What happened to you?" Ginny asked.

"I fell down three little steps," said Mrs. Hobbs. "I won't be able to walk for months. Can you imagine all that trouble over three little steps?"

"That's too bad," said Ginny. "Is there anything I can do to help?"

"Yes, my dear, there is," said Mrs. Hobbs. "Buffy is supposed to go to the vet's tomorrow. It's time for his next shot. Do you think you could drive him there? Heaven knows, I can't!"

Ginny said she could. But she didn't have a pet cage to take Buffy in. She didn't want a little dog loose in her car. Mrs. Hobbs had a cage.

The next day Ginny came to get the dog. She loaded little Buffy into the cage, and off they went to the vet's.

Buffy didn't know what to make of the ride. He had never gone away with anyone but Mrs. Hobbs. Ginny was very glad he was in a cage. She couldn't believe that a little dog could make such a big mess.

Ginny stayed with Buffy while he got his shot. She patted his head as the needle went in. She knew that was just what Mrs. Hobbs would have done if she had been there.

When they got home, Mrs. Hobbs paid Ginny well. That gave Ginny the idea for her pet taxi service. She could take animals anywhere they needed to go. Most of the time, that meant going to the vet or the groomer.

Right away, Ginny put an ad in the newspaper. It said: PET TAXI SERVICE. RIGHT ON TIME. LOW RATES. TENDER LOVING PET CARE. Ginny's phone number was at the end of the ad.

The calls came in. Ginny had found more work for the slow pet-sitting months. She knew that the busy times would come again. She could always turn down pet taxi jobs if she didn't have time.

Then a call came out of the blue. It was from Pipper's owner. Ginny remembered Pipper. He was the cat who would eat only with the dish in line with the door.

"We saw your ad for pet taxi service," said the woman. "You know that Pipper eats a special kind of cat food. But the only place to buy it is 20 miles away. My husband and I work during the day. That makes it hard for us to get there. Could you pick up Pipper's food once a month?"

Ginny was happy to do that. She didn't have to do it at a certain time of day. When she had an extra hour, she could fill it in with a drive to the store.

Before long, Ginny was picking up special food for three customers. She was getting paid three times for the same drive! And she worked out a deal with the pet food store. Now she was even making a little money on the food itself.

Ginny bought pet cages in three sizes. She cleaned them out every time she used them. She didn't want the animals to spread fleas or anything else. And the cages kept the animals in the back of the car—not in the front seat with her.

Late one night Ginny was getting ready for bed. She didn't expect the phone to ring at that hour. It sounded louder than usual.

"This is Mrs. Hobbs, my dear," came the voice. "Something awful has happened to Buffy! He can hardly move and he won't eat. I think he got into some rat poison. I called the vet. He told me what to give Buffy, but I don't have any of it. Can you take him to the doctor right away?"

"I'll be there in a flash," said Ginny.

Buffy lay still in the cage in Ginny's car. From the front seat, Ginny couldn't hear him breathing. But she talked to him all the way to the vet's office. "Hang in there, little guy!" she said. "We're almost there. You're going to be all right!"

She ran five red lights. Her brakes screeched as she pulled into the vet's parking lot.

"We're here, Buffy!" she cried. "Hang in, hang in!"

Ginny picked up the cage and burst into the vet's office. The doctor was waiting. He pushed a pill into Buffy's mouth. He rubbed the dog's throat to help him swallow. When the pill was down, Buffy licked his own nose.

"Now let's hope it works," the doctor said to Ginny.

They waited for what seemed like hours. Really, it was only a few minutes. Then, slowly, Buffy opened his eyes. Ginny could hear him breathing again. She took one of Buffy's paws and rubbed it between her hands.

"It looks like he's out of the woods," the doctor said. "That was a close call."

**CHAPTER 10**

# Animal Friends

"You are so lucky, I can't stand it," Eva was saying to Ginny. "You have your own business. Do you know how great that is? You don't have to worry about being laid off. And you don't have to put up with an unfair boss. I call that lucky!"

"It's not just luck," said Ginny. "I put this thing together and I work hard. And remember—I don't get a paycheck every week. When I don't work, I don't get paid.

I have to work hard for every penny that I make."

"Yes, yes," said Eva. "But still, you're lucky. Things might not have worked out. You might be working at some crummy job again! Why, you even save lives! Your Sam would have been proud of you."

Ginny still got tears in her eyes when she thought of Sam. "All right, I'm lucky," she said. "So why don't you start *your* own business?"

"Actually, I've been thinking about it," Eva said. "You know how I like to groom Roberta. I think maybe I'd like to be a dog groomer."

"Why not?" said Ginny. "Except you might have to clean out dogs' ears. I know how you hate that."

"I could learn to live with it," said Eva. "I mean, can't you just see me as a dog groomer? What fun—I could just clip away all day. Poodles and cocker spaniels and springers and whatever! But no pit bulls. I simply will not touch a pit bull!"

"And you can put that nice perfume on the dogs when they're done," Ginny said.

"And a bow around the neck," Eva added.

"Oh, yes," said Ginny. "Don't forget the bow."

"There's a dog-grooming course at the vo-tech school," Eva said. "It's state-certified and everything. You go to classes for three months. When you finish you're a certified dog groomer. Isn't that great? Can you stand it?"

So that's what Eva did. She kept her day job while she went to school. When she graduated she set up a dog-grooming shop in her basement. It wasn't easy. She had to file all sorts of papers to get a city license. And she had to get a bank loan.

Eva's shop had everything. The main thing was a grooming table. Eva had to buy good clippers, cages, and dryers. Right over the floor drain was a big tub on legs with a hose. Eva loved to wear a bright pink smock when she worked. The dogs seemed to know her by her pink smock.

Eva turned out to be really good at grooming. Ginny told her she was cut out for it. She told Eva to show her work to the vets. They had sent Ginny many new customers. Maybe they would send Eva customers, too.

So Eva gave Roberta the best grooming job she had ever had. That dog looked like a princess and smelled like a rose. Eva was satisfied. She drove Roberta straight to the vet's office.

"Well, isn't she the prettiest girl in town!" said one of the doctors.

Eva got lots of customers from the vet's office. She took out some ads and got calls from them, too. But she got more customers from one person than from any other. Ginny told everyone about Eva. And Eva told everyone about Ginny. The two friends were always a big help to each other.

Ginny's business kept growing and

doing well. About a year later she bought a used van. She kept things in there. And with the van, it was much easier to pick up special food and run the pet taxi.

Soon after that, Ginny moved into her own place. That's when she decided she was ready for a new dog. She had always wanted a black lab. But when the time came, she changed her mind.

One day she drove the van down to the animal shelter. She picked out the cutest mutt she could find. Just for fun, she named him Rover. She loved him right away.

Just like Sam, Rover grew very large but always had a baby face. And just like Sam, Rover loved Ginny back, no matter what.